THE NAILMAKERS'
DAUGHTERS

✦

THE NAILMAKERS'
DAUGHTERS

✦

Emma Purshouse
Iris Rhodes
Marion Cockin

OFFA'S PRESS
2015

First published 2015 by Offa's Press
Ferndale, Pant, Oswestry, Shropshire, SY10 9QD

ISBN: 978-0-9565518-8-7

Typeset in Baskerville Old Face

Designed by Boho Creative, Wolverhampton
Artwork by Linda Nevill
Printed and bound by Lion FPG Limited
Oldbury Road, West Bromwich, B70 9DQ

Contents

THE NAILMAKERS' DAUGHTERS – INTRODUCTION

The Nailmakers' Daughters brings together the voices of three different poets who were born and live in the Black Country. They share with us their observations, over-hearings and memories of lives connected by a deeply rooted affection for their home terrain.

Emma Purshouse, Iris Rhodes and Marion Cockin each pay their dues to the rich history of a region where nail-making was once a thriving cottage industry and 'female blacksmiths' could be found in many communities. Read aloud, their poems capture the rhythms of the Black Country, both in terms of its unique historical dialect and the many distinctive voices it holds today. We are taken on a guided tour of canals, scrapheaps and meadows, and by turn encounter talking flamingos, giant pike, the ghosts of uncles. But although the poems are all grounded in the Black Country they also lift us beyond it with their universal themes of love, loss and hope for the future. We are shown a contemporary world, one with its own new versions of the old nail trade.

Emma Purshouse is a descendant of a nail-maker and lives on a narrow boat. She is a freelance writer and performance poet who has had work widely published in anthologies and magazines. In 2012 her novel *Scratters*, set in the Black Country, was shortlisted for the *Mslexia* unpublished novel prize. She regularly performs at spoken word events and literature festivals across the country.

Iris Rhodes was born in Bradley, Bilston, where she lived before going to college in London in 1960. After living and working in London and Africa for many years she returned to her local roots. She has had a life-long interest in writing and poetry, and had her work widely published.

Marion Cockin was born in Wednesbury. She wrote her first story when she was seven and started writing poetry when she was 16. She qualified as a librarian in 1971 and was an Assistant Librarian for Wolverhampton City until she retired several years ago. She has had poems published in anthologies and national magazines.

Jane Seabourne is an Offa's poet and has published and performed her work extensively. As facilitating editor of this anthology she has worked closely with all three poets to draw together and shape their contributions. She is a teacher and mentor who has lived and worked in the Black Country for many years.

EMMA PURSHOUSE

Contents

Under Class

We are here
in the damp places.
Lift a stone

or a log
and you'll find
us

living in the homes
you wouldn't want
to live in. Scrawling,

scuttling about
our strange business.
Feeding on decay,

fungi, our own
droppings,
your detritus.

You have names for us,
the matey, jokey
cheese bob

and tiggy hog,
industrious tags:-
slaters, butcher-boys,

coffin-chewers.
And then those names
you whisper

behind our
armour plated backs,
the ones that aren't so nice,

the ones with worm
and louse and lice,
that suggest

we might just burrow
underneath your skin
and make it crawl.

Emmie and Arthur's Honeymoon, June 7th 1931

The earth really did move for them
in that B & B in Bewdley.
6.1 on the Richter scale,
the bedroom positively rocked.
Elsewhere, chimneys tumbled
and Doctor Crippen's head fell off
at Madame Tussauds in London.

Shaken they scurried back to Sedgley,
never again to venture anywhere
further than a bike or scooter ride
away. No good could come
from not being home in time to light
the greenhouse paraffin lamps
or cover the canary.   No good at all.

Only child

thwacks
ten
nis
ball
ag
ainst
house
wall
for
ow
uh
af
ter
ow
uh
til
fed
up
dad
takes
and
con
fis
cates
racqu
et
to
stop
rack
et

Things I Learned from my Maternal Grandfather:-

the value of canals,
where the best blackberries are found,
that pigs' trotters are edible,
that I am like a bibble in a can,
that if you cut up a golf ball with a hacksaw
    the results can be interesting,
the names of the flowers,
to tell Jehovah's Witnesses you're a Buddhist
    so they will leave you be,
the smell of incense,
words like glede and saftness
    and that cardigans are ganzies,
the keeping out of oss roads,
the smell of oil paints and linseed,
how to fire an air rifle,
    how not to clean it when it's loaded,
        how shooting at imaginary burglars in the dark
            will cause holes in greenhouse windows,
double digging,
to always plant potatoes on Good Friday,
where to find the fossils
    and the interesting graves,
that all books are special,
how to play the mouth organ
    badly,
how to play the penny whistle
    badly,
how to play the spoons
    badly,
how to play the bones
    badly,
how to play whist
    well,

how to take snuff,
  Back of yer ond,
    doh tell yer mother,
how to take the peel from an apple
  in one long curl,
how the steam engine at the waterworks operates,
that bikes should be polished,
how to sleep in the afternoon,
that you can never have too many
  clocks,
  watches,
  radios,
how to make garden fires,
  how to deal with neighbours who react badly to garden fires,
    how everyone in the street should have a nickname,
how not to ask people how they are in case they tell you,
how upstairs on the front seat of the bus is the best way to travel,
how not to fix an electric fire in winter,
how to miss someone.

bibble – small stone or pebble
glede – cinder, ember.
saftness – stupidity or frivolous things
ganzy – cardigan
oss – horse
Keep out the oss road – a way of telling someone to take care.
ond – hand
doh – don't

Things I Learned from my Maternal Grandmother:-

suffering in silence
(see previous poem).

Things I Learned from my Paternal Grandmother:-

licorice imps should be carried
        in a gold case,
always leave your hat on
        when you babysit.

Things I Learned from my Paternal Grandfather:-

a slim volume of poetry
        is one way to communicate after death.
A signature holds no clues.

Machine Parts

(for Trissie Lavender)

That's how it wuz frum mornin' 'til night,
Betty put 'em together, got 'em jus' right
and me with me air gun ar screwed the screws tight.

Then some other bugger'd tek the thing off
for somebody else to dip in red ock.
Then it wuz onto a belt to where it wuz hot

so Hilda could purrem to dry on the floo-wer
til they wuz all done and dusted and off aht the doo-wer.
All of ower lives were spent mekin moo-wer

and ne'rn a one of uz had a clue what they wuz.
In this life yow'm alloted yow duz what you duz
and that, ower kid, well that's jus' how it guz.

red ock – red oxide

How Bilston and Battersea Enamel Seconds are Created

Dot, dot, beak, beak,
I load my brush
dot, dot, beak, beak,
from the pot
dot, dot, beak, beak,
of mustard yellow
dot, dot, beak, beak,
paint flowers
dot, dot, beak, beak,
centres only
dot, dot, beak, beak,
and the birds
dot, dot, beak, beaks,
only.
Dot, dot, beak, beak.
pass on the lid
dot, dot, beak, beak,
to the girl next door
dot, dot, beak, beak,
she's better than me
dot, dot, beak, beak,
she's allowed to swirl
dot, dot, beak, beak,
she paints a leaf
dot, dot, beak, beak,
a tendril, a curl
dot, dot, beak, beak
in emerald green
dot, dot, beak, beak,
she's glamorous
dot, dot, beak, beak
and not cack handed

dot, dot, beak, beak,
like me.
Dot, dot, beak, beak,
I wish I was her
dot, dot, beak, blob,
oh god.

Bilston and Battersea Enamels - a company famous for producing
enamelled boxes and other trinkets.

Star Taxis – Captain's Log, 10pm to 6am

From inside her cage
at base
she stares out
at
venus-yellow walls,
at
the piece of
space junk
sitting in the plastic chair
shoveling handfuls
of Major's chips
(which glow brighter than Sirius)
into
the black hole of his mouth
as he awaits transportation
to Moxley.

She rides out the lull,
willing it to ring.

And suddenly
she has lift off,
star after *star* after *star.*

An explosion
of *stars.*
The receiver burns white hot.

She's womaning the phones
bringing back
the bingo babes
from planet Mecca

in the faraway galaxy
of Wednesbury.

She's maintaining radio contact
with the
taxi-nauts
as they orbit
the town
like satellites.

She's adopting an
advisory capacity,
Hang on a bit for her, Raj;
'er int too good with stairs.

She's handling
the meteor shower
that pours in from
Robin II,
putting a rocket under
the Bradley boy
who's been on
Betelgeuse
for far too long,
This is a no smoking area!
Tek it outside, space cadet!
He won't be burning up
on re-entry.

Bilston,
she doesn't have a problem.
Challenger, Columbia,

not on this watch.
She is mission control
and for five beautiful hours
the universe revolves
around her.

By three fifteen
the ticker tape parade is over.
She's brought the heroes
safely home.

Sentinel,
she holds her post.
Waiting in the dark
for signs of life,
those straggler UFOs
that may yet still appear
in the light year
between four and six
when she prefers to think
she's not alone
with her thoughts
and the occasional crackle of static.

Star Taxis – a Bilston Taxi firm
Major's – a very popular Bilston chip shop
Robin II – a live music venue in Bilston

Vera Considers Life and the Universe

I wuz areadin' this book, yuh know, on the universe and all that, an' I sez to him, I sez, *John, did yow know that 96% of the universe is missing? Missing?* he sez like he aye really listenin'. *Yes Missing. Doh yow find that a bit, yuh know, worrying like? Maybe, John, maybe we'm like the Jona Lewies of spairce.* He puts the pairper dahn then and he sez, *Yow what? Maybe,* I sez again, *We'm like the Jona Lewies of spairce. Yuh know, John, like we'm shut in the kitchen at the big spairce party and everythin', all the best bits am gooin' on in the rest of the plairce. Maybe in the bits we cor see, in all that dark matter and in all that dark energy, maybe that's where it all happens.* Then he starts humming Stop the Cavalry and I sez, *No, John, that aye the song, that aye the song at all.* And he sez, *Wos fuh dinna?* And I sez, *Chickin!* And that wuz as far as it got last Sunday for me and astrophysics, that was as far as it got.

It's Her Regional Dish

so every Thursday from the butcher's shop –
red quarry tiles and sawdust – she buys
a bag, soaks them overnight in water,
adds one tab bicarbonate of soda.
By Friday tea the kitchen window's steamed
from a two hour smelting process. They've gone
from bullet hard to the consistency of slurry
and are ready to be forked from plate to gob –
coke to stoke a furnace. One night a week
M & S and Waitrose are forsaken for
this feast. A taste she'd claim to be *acquired,*
a taste of what she was and is. They turn
her bowels and vowels inside out in a blaze
of ritual indigestion. Grey paes – no bacon.

Flamingos in Dudley Zoo

Special ay we? He starts again,
always mithering with questions.
Great being a flamingo ay it?
Always bletherin' on he is.
I like havin' feathers, doh yow?
No different when he was an egg.
Tap, tap, tappety tap. No peace
to be had. He stands on one leg,
What was it like in the owd days, nan?
Doh half remind me of his dad.
Aye got the heart to tell him
as how it's always bin like this,
the pond by the gates, the faces,
the chair-lift soaring overhead,
us sky-watching, pale with envy.
When I'm growed up I'll fly the nest
to Chile or the South of France.
His enthusiasm's killing me.
Yow best talk proper, chick. I say,
or yow wo get nowhere in this world
like me. He squawks. So pink he is,
so pink. My wicked tongue holds back.
I shut my beak. I keep it zipped.
He doh know our wings am clipped.

mithering – pestering or worrying
blethering – to talk incessantly or to talk nonsense

Tat

Rusty padlocks, keys, a hulk
of broken chain twisted out of kilter,
nails long enough to skewer

a foot to the floor and hold it.
All souvenirs from trips I've taken.
The Black Country Museum bits

are scavenged pieces,
picked up as demonstrators
of old trades turned their backs

or were distracted by a question.
That there's a cut-dipping find,
a boatman's windlass hauled up

dripping from a lock. Spinning
on the end of a rope, clinging
to my sea-searcher magnet.

This copper pot. Floundering
in dredgers' mud it was. Wide mouthed,
fat bellied as any carp. A beaut!

The photo tucked behind that mound
of swarf's a Dudley-Dowell I snapped
in Devon, the last week of July

or first in August.   Went by train.
That hammer there's for breaking glass.
The best bit about my going

was the coming back. That pull for home
tempered by a glimpse of scrap
the first this side of New Street.

Dudley-Dowell - In recent years The Black Country Bugle
encouraged people to send in photos of Black Country
ironwork that had been spotted at different places around the
world. A number of those were made by a Cradley Heath
company called Dudley Dowell Ltd.

If There Was Ever Any Danger of Being Dazzled by Your Own Brilliance

E'yar, cocker.
She greets me with a shout.
This come for yow yesterday
when yow was aht.
Brown A4 envelope is jiggled
like a low budget puppet
above the eight foot fence.
OK, I yell, *Chuck it.*
And she does. Up
and over.

As it descends
I catch it.

Anything good? she pries
through a gap in the larch lap.
I stand - no cap just dressing gown -
waving parchment paper.
Ohh, MA certificate.
That's nice aye it, pet.
S'pose there's no news
on the job front though as yet?

Then and Now

In cramped and sooty caverns
we ply our trade
to the clink and tinkle of hammers
and the smell of fire
for eight shillings a week.
Horse, frost, gate, boat,
rose head square, rose sharp,
rose flat, rose clench,
spikes
is what this work entails.
Our trade is nails.

In spacious well lit salons
we ply our trade
to the snaky hiss of compressed air,
the smell of acetone
for minimum wage.
Gel, gem, stripe, flick,
long squared, short squared, round,
stiletto, squoval, French tip,
oval
is what this work entails.
Our trade is nails.

In Cramped and Sooty Caverns – the title of a book by Dr Michael Hall
about the nail-makers of Birmingham, Bromsgrove and the Black
Country explored through the novels of Francis Brett Young.

IRIS RHODES

Contents

Once Upon a Time

A scent, a sound, a nuance of the air,
The small things take you back
Where in the land of *once upon a time*
The things once commonplace
Seem strange and rare.
In seconds, time revolves, decades dissolve.
Once upon a time still in your mind,
Still there.

Found Object in Old House

Newspaper wrapped –
A cobwebbed cylinder
Tucked in a corner
Of a dusty room.

The paper shreds,
Proclaims a date – 1914 –
And news of war.

Inside – a parasol.
The bamboo handle creaks.
Spines flex, waxed circle spreads –
A spray of blossom
Bright as hope,
Fragile as happiness,
Unfurls and blooms.

Return of Walter Rhodes from the 1914-18 War

When he came back,
It was not along the road
Festooned with banners
And friends and neighbours
In their Sunday best
To cheer their hero home.

It was past the canal
With its slow glide of swans
And the deep cool green
Of its remembered smell.

Then through the fields of willow-herb
Where, stroking fragile flowers,
He longed to lie among the purple spires
And sleep, blanketed with silence,
The dreamless miracle
Of safe and empty sky.

On Platform Three

Strange in his rough uniform,
Hair convict-short,
Neck white
And young,
And vulnerable.
He will not meet my eyes,
Stands tough and awkward –
Needs to be a man among his mates,
Not some sad woman's son.
I want to creep under his skin, and there
Take to myself the bullets, shrapnel, bombs,
The harm may come under a foreign sky.
I want to hold him tight.
Instead I touch his sleeve,
Through fingertips pour all my love and care,
Then turn and walk away.

Flashback – 1947

Against the chip-shop wall
He leans on crutches, raging profanities.
The children tease, then run away,
Breathless with their own daring.
The grown-ups leave him be –
Talk of the bright-eyed boy they knew –
The tall, strong lad he was,
How he could run,
Came first in Bradley marathons –
How hard a worker down the mine,
How caring and how good a son
And how his voice was clear and true
In the church choir
In 1939.

Looking Back

Winter long ago –
Inside the window panes
The swirling feathered patterns on the glass,
Lino like a skating rink,
And the wrapped brick cooling in the bed.
The ice in chamber pots, unfreezing on the hob
Before the chattering run to outside lavatory –
Cold draught under the door,
Newspaper hung in chilly squares on string.

Waiting for the snow to fall –
Exhilaration when it came at last, and stayed,
And trying not to spoil the loveliness
With the first footsteps, tiny though they were.
Making the snowman, taller than myself,
Pride in its completion,
Sadness, when the big boys knocked it down.
White playgrounds where the bravest rode the slides
Arms stretched, flying without fear –
And watching, envying their courage –
Wishing for a piece of it.

Icicles like lollies in red hands,
Soaked woollen gloves
And going home to wet clothes in the kitchen,
The smell of steam and gas,
Blue flame escaping from the mantle gauze.
Looking out as darkness fell
And waiting for more snow –
And all the tomorrows yet to come.

Sticky Buds

Nothing more lovely than a tree, she said,
Arranging twigs in a glass vase –
Miss Haig, my teacher with the shiny shoes.
I puzzled, till the tight buds swelled
And broke into a green intensity –
And then I understood, and I, a seven-year-old,
Was glad my teacher with the shiny shoes
Had shared her thoughts
With me.

Pothouse Bridge, Bradley

Towpath
And the scrape of metalled hooves
On cobble stones.
Harness jingle,
Dip and splash of rope
And the blow of snorting horses
Mist grey in the morning cold
And the children, on their way to school,
Leaning over Pothouse Bridge
To wave at barge men –
Envying their freedom,
Their castles and roses –
The otherness
Of their secret lives.

The Queen's Ballroom, Wolverhampton

Do you remember
Queuing up, head-scarfed against the wind,
Toes pinched already in your pointed shoes.
Do you remember
Powder rooms – the elbowing for mirror space,
The burdened handbags and the borrowing of combs,
The barbed-wire hairdos fixed with choking sprays.
Do you remember
Ring-stitched bras and straps with safety pins,
Hauling suspenders, straightening seams, last minute
preens
And squirts, obligatory, of scents with hopeful names.
The check-in – numbers round the wrist – and then the fear
No-one would walk through Woodbine smoke
To claim you for a dance,
Although you'd saved for months
For the new dress, earrings to match.
Do you remember
Glitterballs and glamour
And transformed girls out looking for romance
And lads in unaccustomed suits
Just looking.
Do you remember
Getting drunk on Babycham
And the bright lights swirling –
And somehow getting home on the last bus –
And your Dad, on the front doorstep,
Looking at his watch?

Silver Shoes

I watched her as she burned
The silver shoes, for warmth,
And wondered if the memory
Of her wedding day came back
As the flames caught
And cracked and blistered shining heels.

Her face was turned away.
I could not read her thoughts,
Know if the burning caused regret –
Relief perhaps? A protest
Or a kind of sacrifice, was it?

I stretched my hands to fire –
Glad of the warmth,
Sad for the burning of the silver shoes.

Reversal

You held me when the prowling wolf
Snapped at the yellow ducks along my cot
With teeth as sharp as knives.
When I was ill
You lit a fire in the front room
And fed me chicken soup.

Now, like a child afraid,
You whimper at your nameless fears.

God help us all,
I am your mother now.
Hold tight, my love, I will not let you go.
We walk the rope,
The wolves howl down below.

Starlings from the National Theatre Balcony

And oh – the swirl and swoop –
The looping of the loop –
Kinetic curve
And structured sweep and swerve,
The coiling, curling harmony,
The verve of liquid flight –
As watchers on the balcony
Commit the aerial tracery
To memory –
At sunset,
In the slow fade of the light.

Chameleon Lady on the London/Euston Line

Time and the train speed on
Over the hidden mineshafts
And the graves of ancestors.

Passing the castle on the hill
She folds her London skin into her case,
Takes out her mask again.

She is well-practised in this change –
An actress consummate,
Respecting her own skills.
Forty-odd years perfect the ease,
The seamless slide into another life.

No-one applauds the role.
No paparazzi cameras flash,
Record the transformed woman stepping down –
Or her strange smile,
When, at the station rank,
The taxi driver asks:
Where are you going, Bab?
Not knowing her true name means *rainbow,*
That every time she makes this trip,
She leaves behind her colours
On the train.

My Garden in Africa

Dar es Salaam, Tanzania

All night rain clatters
On tin roof,
Rhythmic as sticks on a steel drum.
Ripe mangoes fall
Moongold and shining in the dark.
At six o'clock the garden steams,
Palms arch and frangipani wafts
Like incense in a church.
On the wet path
Blue starlings squabble
Over fallen fruit.

The Bat Tree at Sunset

A slow ride home,
Sky heavy as a canopy,
Red silk, gold fringed over the palms.
The sun falls like a stone
Behind the backdrop of the hills.
Cicadas chorus
And the bats leave black branches,
Erupt, wings clapping,
Into the theatre of the night.

The Haunting

In the dry seasons,
Waiting for the rains to come –
The dark ghost of a scent –

Limpopo banks, Zambesi Falls,
White beaches and the quiet sea,
It followed me, but where it came from
Was a mystery, 'til, decades on,
I knew that it belonged
Under a canal bridge, back home.

Where sweating navvies shifted rock and clay,
Where weary miners rested from their day,
Where lovers found their freedom and their privacy.
Where children, with their nets and jars,
Peered into soup-thick water for their prey,
Stirring the secret, clutching weeds,
Heedless of punishment to be.

Where vapour, green as primal swamps,
Would wreathe throughout the years
The phantom smell of childhood and of history.

The Conservatory, West Park, Wolverhampton

Grown massive in the heat
The plants revert, take on their tropic size,
And curved and spiked, become a Rousseau paradise
As stripes and spots embellish leaves and orchids glow,
Suggest the widespread wings of butterflies.
Here, in the steaming quiet, fanciful,
One might forget reality – imagine watching eyes,
The shift of purple shadow, rasp of claws on bark,
The warning shriek of monkeys
And the fluid lope of jungle cat,
As time stands still, it seems – transformed, enclosed,
In the Conservatory, West Park.

Travellers' Horses

No Stubbs' Arabians these,
The ambling piebalds
Sturdy in the road
As car horns blare
And red-faced motorists
Bawl out their repertoire of oaths.

Profanities ignored,
The horses claim the ground
As though on ancient prairies
Where, with their hooves unshod,
They range where grass is sweet,
Where clean wind blows
And only eagles call.

The Rocket Pools, Bradley

They used to say the pools were bottomless
And giant monster pike lurked in their depths,
Ageless and cruel and big enough
To drag trespassing children to their death.

It was a weekend treat
To walk surrounding fields,
Pick buttercups, spot dragonflies,
Where clover masked the reek of factory smoke
And the calm pools were green and deep.

Now houses crowd
Where once the wild flowers grew.
At the pool's rim, the lager cans adorn the reeds.
On shopping trolleys, half-submerged,
The moorhens roost.

The fishermen sit still
Among the debris of their meals
And plastic bags float, lily-like,
Above the silent, waiting pike.

Black Country Aubade

Mist rises from canals,
Reveals the fields
Where dreaming horses stand
And a lone walker whistles,
Strides, knee-deep in purple willow-herb,
Past the brown bones, the rusting ribs,
The ghosts of factories.

an aubade is a poem or music appropriate to the dawn

MARION COCKIN

Contents

The Wednesbury Mangle Theory

It all began
with the mangle
in the cupboard
with the undoing of the nut
with the shock
of the clanging of the handle
on the red tiled floor.
The *om* of curiosity
rang out unmelodiously
like Galileo scraping on his plate.

Newton had an apple.
We had the mangle handle
and its repeated falling
to the ground.

This began
a spreading circle
of undoing things
pressing buttons
pulling random levers
turning keys
in hidden doors.

The chaos theory first discovered
not in the 1960s
but by a mangle in a cupboard
in 1954.

Galileo, when scratching images of sunspots on a varnished copper plate,
discovered patterns in the vibration.

George and Cal are Dancing

The day dad died,
he saw George and Cal dancing,
in the corner of the bedroom,
above the print of gilly flowers.

Did he hear the music?
Did they wear
grey overcoats and trilbies
and shoes polished to a glorious shine?
Did they have a pint of mild apiece
and hand out their humbugs
smelling of stale tobacco
from dusty jacket pockets?

I remember dancing
with George, or was it Cal?
Uncles who taught me how to waltz.
We danced on our front room carpet
patterned with red daisies
placed just a step apart.

The day dad died,
mom took the sweeper
and scrubbed at the carpet
to hide the sound of leaving
from the empty room above.

Apple Green

It's April, the fields are apple green,
the apple green from rows of paints
on wooden desks.
The yellow is always smeared with brown,
the unsatisfactory red is cold,
the blue is ultramarine,
impossible for skies.

But apple green is perfect
for meadows with dots of daffodils,
for sunshine woods and beanstalk leaves,
for giant's boots and playing fields.

I sit up straight with folded arms,
toes clenched in patent leather shoes,
hoping to catch the teacher's gaze.
My tight lips curve into a smile
when I am chosen,
to paint the trees
on the playground frieze
apple green.

The Sacred Way

Break stones
to find their hidden colours.
Drench with sun-warmed water
to make their reds and browns shine.
Bless the rusty tin,
line with bright green leaves,
put each shattered pebble in its place.
Carry gently through the arch
where petals fall.

Circle the flower bed
at least three times.
Stop at the spire of runner beans.
Walk down the secret path
lined with sky-blue delphiniums.
Reach the sacred apple tree,
lay the treasure there
and sing a half-remembered hymn.

Return a different way
and see the rockery gleaming white
in the evening sun.

Pussy Willow Time

The willow's bare
but weaves its branches
like a map across the sky
or a mass of wires
that lift and steal some sounds
from somewhere else.

It's pussy willow time,
mom says.
Just to please her
we find them
peeking through the rusty fence
in the field by Barlow's yard.

The horse looks on.
When we've finished cutting twigs,
we pull up chunks of grass and weed
and offer them on open palms
as we've been shown.

We wave the whipping branches,
play horse across the tip
but take care not to hurt
the precious silky cushions.
We take them home,
proud and pleased.

She puts them on the sill
behind the sink
in the old chipped vase.

She watches as the twigs
light up with leaves.

Common

Grey pays and bacon
fruit bowls in windows
plaster alsatians
faggots and chicklings
fried brains and tripe

tap dance and ballet
(makes your kids brassy)
flouncy net dresses
and smooth satin sashes
petunias – all colours
kids with no knickers.

Women in trousers
with red nails and lipstick
smoking or drinking,
shouting or whistling.

ITV programmes
the flea pit, Rialto
pop from the pop van
live chicks from the rag man
never-never, hire purchase
catalogue bargains
men in their undies
playing cards on Sundays
bottles on tables
prize winning dahlias.

But worst of the lot
is the secondary mod.
No 11 plus failures.
Not in this house.

Chicklings are chitterlings a dish made with pig's intestine

Women I Live With

They've all visited my hippocampus
and after many, many readings
made the frontal cortex
swinging on the synapses
swimming in the fizz of serotonin
having lots of fun.
They're still here, bouncing on the myelin
eating sweets of glutamate
to make their memory stick.
They wrap my nervy bundles
in suffocating blankets
and feed them all with cocoa
while I'm in REM sleep.

There's Jo and Amy, Meg and Beth,
Katy, Clover and Rose Red.
Wendy, Jinks and Nurse Sue Barton.

And here she comes
charging on her white horse
leaping across the neurons
causing havoc with her voices
her armour making sparks,
causing some short circuits
and some minor little shocks
perhaps a cluster migraine
or an irritating twitch.
She is *my* Joan of Arc
with her private line to God.

Sparrows

Back then our days began
with sparrows squabbling in the eaves.
After breakfast, we showered the path
with crumbs of unsliced white
and gaudy battenburg.
The sparrows filled the yard
and fought for cake.
A lucky brown bibbed male
got marzipan.

Over the years
the sparrows left,
not all at once
but one by one.

Last summer,
we found them
in tenement flats
of piled high twigs
below the white stork's nest
in northern Greece.

The Road from Nairobi

We passed the British Camp, just left Nairobi,
and there they were, all dressed up in Sunday best
in the shimmering blistering summer heat,
dust free in glowing coats and heavy hats.

Families strolled down the hill from church
past the Saviour's Hotel and Trust God Shoes
to scattered metal shacks, circumnavigated
by goats and sheep.

We drove on, talked of Sundays past.

In church, you fought over marbles,
almost burst with giggles in the wooden pews.
You played forbidden Sunday football,
scrubbed bloodied knees with spit and hanky,
wiped muddied shoes to conceal the sin.

I soaked up the stories
of noble Daniel in the lion's den,
pre-technicolor Joseph and his dreams
Ruth gleaning barley in the sun scorched fields
and comic strips of saintly missionaries
selling their gods to save the world.

Crocodile Bar – Samburu Lodge

They meant it when they said
Crocodile Bar.
As we drink our chilled beer
the crocs lie watching us
armed to the teeth
the bastard slitty-eyed creatures.
I think I will buy
enough crocodile bags
to fill the plane.

They know we're talking about them
but do they care?
Their collective memory
converses with dinosaurs.

They slide back into the river
and wait
for the weighing of our souls.

How We Found Ourselves with a Carpet in Marrakech

We should not have been surprised
when they found an unmarked door
and led us up the lamp-lit stairs
to rooms stacked high with carpets.

They sat us down and served mint tea.
The first glass as gentle as life.
The second glass as strong as love.
The third glass as bitter as death.

So now we have Solomon's carpet,
green for retribution and resurrection.
It took the king, his throne, his soldiers,
all his women across mountains and seas.
It lies, a paradise garden of deception
on our front room floor.

The Writing on the Wall

When you strip away the layers you will find
graffiti on a bedroom wall.
Time travels behind paper
reminds you that in '92 Kate said
Hello to everyone, especially Ste.
A comic cowboy draws his gun
(willies were enormous then,
just look at the size of that!).
Underneath –
a strange request concerning strawberry jam.

Dave (it was his bedroom after all)
signed everywhere and so did
Rebecca, Guns and Roses, Megadeth.
Bernie was there neatly up a corner
and so was Ammo, Jonesie, Ste and Kate.

When the plasterers come,
it will all be put to bed.
Twenty years skimmed away.
Well, it's just writing on the wall.
Not weighed, numbered and divided.
Just Kate loved Ste.

Nasturtiums for Logan

You tore the packet
leaving a white mountain edge
across the orange and green
of flowers and leaves.
You poured seeds
into your hand,
dropping three which rolled
and found a home
in the crevice between
the paving stones.

We'll plant some here
and here against the wall.
You pressed the seeds
into the sweet soil.

Next time you came
a small green umbrella
had pushed its way
to see you.
I think perhaps
you were not impressed.
You went indoors.

Next time you came
nasturtium leaves
made a forest of green plates.
You gave a sympathetic smile
and *very nice.*
You went indoors.
I sighed.

But come August
when the sun burned down
on the orange wall
and the orange flowers
bellowed their brilliance
you said,
Wow!

The Times I Think that You Have Died

While I sit waiting
in restaurants,
I look at your absent chair
and ponder over a glass of wine
what to wear at your funeral.

An empty space at tai chi class
when you've just popped out to the loo.
We've struggled through the form
three times before you return.
And in between the shaky moves,
I've remarried twice.

The climax of the film,
the closing of the play,
I turn and find that you are gone.
I contemplate your death again
and miss the point.
When you return and ask what happened
I cannot say, you died.
You can still be there
and die beside me.
Your head falls to my shoulder
in hot concert halls.
Like a mother
I check your breathing.
And even worse
(though I'm glad you're still alive)
I correct you snores
with nudges in the ribs.

Please when you do die,
if it's before me of course,
don't let it be sitting on a toilet seat
or slumped to Ravel's Bolero
or the Planet Suite.
Let it be somewhere
unpractised.

Close Friends

In ways we are alike
closely corresponding
here and there.

So when we fight
it is a close finish.
Our close reasoning leaves
no gaps.

You can be close
but there again you're male.
Your thoughts are secret
and do not fall about
making loud noises
for all to hear.

I can be close but have
to hold back your spending ways,
before you throw our fortunes
to the wind.

We're close, we're very near
we share a bed, a house,
a car.

We are a close texture
no light between
our warp and weft.

So I guess as much
as anyone can be,
we're friends.
Close friends.

I Have Made a Room For Us

I have made a room for us from rock
and ferns and frilly hawthorn leaves, clover,
creeping cinquefoil and dandelion clocks.
The windows only welcome clear blue skies.
The deep armchairs are raptor shadow grey.
The walls are layers of wrinkled stone and
from their craggy tops the peregrines watch.

I scatter flower seeds in the spring
watered by spills of coffee, tea and wine
and April showers of biscuit crumbs and ash.

Summer makes our room a bed of musk-rose,
scarlet poppies, marjoram and thyme.
Trees breathe quietly and shelter us from rain.

Autumn turns our room from green to brown
with mellow sunlight splashed with gold and red.

In winter the snow floats down as feathers
dark branches hold silver leaves of frost
yet our room is warm as roasted chestnuts
and the blazing fire will last until the spring.

ACKNOWLEDGEMENTS

Emma Purshouse
Machine Parts, How Bilston and Battersea Enamel Seconds are
Created, Star Taxis – Captain's Log – 10pm to 6am, It's Her
Regional Dish, Flamingos in Dudley Zoo, If There was Ever
Any Danger of Being Dazzled by Your Own Brilliance, Then
and Now were developed for a performance of Black Country
Poetry at the Arena Theatre in Wolverhampton as part of
the Black Country Echoes Festival in November 2014. Vera
Considers Life and the Universe was written and performed as
part of the multi-media show, E-X-P-A-N-D-I-N-G:- the history
of the universe in 45 minutes.

Iris Rhodes
On Platform Three first published in *Sunrise Over Machu Pichu*,
WomenWords Books.
My Garden in Africa first published in *New Writings from
Wolverhampton*, Wolverhampton Libraries.